MY SHOES ARE KILLING ME

*Robyn Sarah*

# MY SHOES ARE KILLING ME

*poems*

BIBLIOASIS • WINDSOR, ONTARIO

FIRST EDITION
Second printing, November 2015

Library and Archives Canada Cataloguing in Publication
Sarah, Robyn, author
    My shoes are killing me / Robyn Sarah.

Poems.
Issued in print and electronic formats.
ISBN 978-1-77196-013-7 (pbk.).--ISBN 978-1-77196-014-4 (ebook)

    I. Title.

PS8587.A3765M92 2015        C811'.54        C2014-907965-6
                                            C2014-907966-4

The poem 'it is not in great acts' is reprinted with permission of Les Éditions du Noroît from *Le tamis des jours: poèmes choisis* (2007), a bilingual edition of poems by Robyn Sarah with French translations by Marie Frankland.

Biblioasis acknowledges the ongoing financial support of the Government of Canada through the Canada Council for the Arts, Canadian Heritage, the Canada Book Fund; and the Government of Ontario through the Ontario Arts Council and the Ontario Media Development Corporation.

Canada Council for the Arts    Conseil des arts du Canada    Canadian Heritage    Patrimoine canadien

ONTARIO ARTS COUNCIL
CONSEIL DES ARTS DE L'ONTARIO
50 YEARS OF ONTARIO GOVERNMENT SUPPORT OF THE ARTS
50 ANS DE SOUTIEN DU GOUVERNEMENT DE L'ONTARIO AUX ARTS

Edited by Eric Ormsby
Copy-edited by Emily Donaldson
Typeset and designed by Kate Hargreaves

PRINTED AND BOUND IN CANADA

# CONTENTS

Notes
Acknowledgements

*For Jodi,*
*who gives me courage*

## IN THE SLANT LIGHT

On a grassy bank under a willow tree
I fell asleep pillowed in an elbow of summer,
and woke to see snow falling.

It is too late now for many things,
too late for so many things.
The sun barely skirts the treetops
before beginning its downward arc.
Across the still air, sporadic hammer-sounds
ring out, metal on metal—men on scaffolds,
men on ladders in the slant light,
battening down the hatches for winter.

What happened to noon, high noon?
There used to be noon.
Time is evaporating like a tide pool,
leaving its stranded flotsam, a cipher
scribbled across the sand. Debris
of our days—we had better look to it.
What to discard, and what pass on?
What yet to hoard to keep us warm?

Something to dig around in.
Something to chew on.
As the future shrinks, the past
looms larger, the past
is compost, is pemmican.

# A BOX OF OLD FAMILY PHOTOS

Here we see our
selves in transit.
Time's the terrain.
Here are our sundry
faces, lost familiars,
the parade of we-were-onces,
bygones of the mirror
half remembered,
hardly believed in, now.

Precious beyond accounting
is this salvage, yet how
unaccountably it takes us
when it takes us unawares:
where are those years?

The past is hazardous
as well as treasurehouse.

## READING MARIANNE MOORE ON A TRAIN BETWEEN COBOURG AND KINGSTON

At first I thought the past
must have alighted on my wrist,
and it was neither owl nor moth,
but word misread.
It pointed me my path.

We passed a faery forest.
Trees dipped overnight in mist
and sugared with a thin fur of frost
held masses of lacy twigwork up
to the sun. The snow cover, further on,
was like a threadbare cotton blanket
thrown down over the fields—it showed
the contours of the ground beneath,
furrow and stone, with tufts of grass
and weedstalk poking through.
The book lay open in my lap.

Later, two dogs stood far apart,
lonely and wagging on a snow field,
and for a long fast stretch
the train whistle wailed a blues chord,
inverted sixth.

I thought I heard it blast
that misread word,

the Past      the Past      the Past

## WHAT TIME IS IT?

*Snapshot: A two-year-old boy, chubby, serious, with bangs cut across his forehead like a girl's, stands on the front walk—a little boy in short pants with buttons on the sides and suspenders over a blouse with a sailor collar. In the background can be seen a nursery evergreen, a baby spruce not much taller than he is, plunked down in the middle of the lawn like a painted tree in a toy village.*

I saw the tree from the bus window the other day. It is magnificent, spreading lush feathery branches over the front yard, towering above the roof of that duplex with its Tudor-style façade, the first home I clearly remember living in. The boy I have not seen since our sister's wedding (her third) seven years ago. At that time I had also not seen him for several years. I was surprised to find him greying, though I tried not to show it. He is the younger of us two. By now I have begun to grey as well.

Time picks clean the bones of the present, then like a sea catches them up and transforms them, twisting and silvering and eating away the rough edges.

And we go on creaming the night face. We wake each day and strap the time on our wrists. We have lists of things to do and get. A life of preparation, a life of errands. Laying the table over and over for a feast that never materializes. What time is it? What time is it? It's time for us to sit down and eat, even without fine linen, even without candles. And no matter if the feast is a chunk of dry bread.

## MY SHOES ARE KILLING ME

*(a poem in nine movements)*

i  YOU COULD ALMOST UNDERSTAND

It was the beginning of dwindle.
Even the ink was stingy.
The doctor was mortal.

Some of the stickiness had worn off
the things we had to do.
For a while they still clung, like bits
of wet Scotch tape. Some washed away
in rains that came. We let them go.

Rain was falling through my
burnt gazebo.

One morning I thought I saw the last
unevaporated dewdrop in the grass,
among the little shaggy heads of white clover
(second-growth, end-of-summer clover)
and I said *Where is my trampoline?*
I said *Where is my toboggan?*
*Where are my monkey bars*, I said,
and *Where is my roller skate key?*
Where is my brain, was the real question.
It seemed to have wandered off.

Then the lights went down and suddenly
it was a movie about trees, no, not *about*,
it was a movie of trees,
it was a movie of trees moving
in wind, and of branches heaving
in wind, and the sound
was of wind soughing in branches

and of great rushes of wind in leaves
(the sound dying down then starting up again
at some other spot in the wall of greenery)
and there was no other sound
but the layers of whoosh and wind-rush
in the lashing wall of greenery,
no other sound but what the trees
were saying to each other in the wind
in their own language,
and there were no subtitles,
but you could almost understand
what the trees were saying.


ii  A YELLOWING

It was the beginning of dwindle.

I was imagining a museum
of dead sounds, a repository
for the lost soundtrack
of daily life, horse-clop on city streets,
tinkle of winter sleighbells, thunder of coal
down coal chutes, the peck and clack
of manual typewriters (*zing*
of their carriages and *ting*
of their carriage bells),
clock-tick and clock-chime,
the milkman's jangling carry-crates,
noon whistles, squeak of clothesline pulleys,
"Chopsticks" on parlour pianos,
five o'clock carillon tunes
and radio jingles advertising
products long gone from shelves near you,
*You'll wonder where the yellow went*
*when you brush your teeth with Pepsodent,*

(only you won't any more,
you will not wonder, for
the yellow is ever with us,
yellow the colour of dwindle
and dwindle a yellowing
of pages, kitchen ceilings, bathroom tiles,
net curtains and Venetian blinds,
and Indian cottons stowed in trunks,
and Kodachrome in albums,
thinning skin in elbow creases,
thickening footsole calluses,
our jaundiced hopes
like flat champagne
in last night's unwashed glasses)

And I said *Where is my trampoline?*
I said *Where is my toboggan?*
*Where are my monkey bars*, I said.

And I wanted to write subtitles
for a movie of trees rustling in wind.


iii  DOMINION OBSERVATORY TIME SIGNAL

> *"The beginning of the long dash following ten seconds of
> silence marks exactly one o'clock, Eastern Standard Time."*

*Beep. Beep. Beep. Beep. Beep. Beep.          Beeeeeeeeeep.*

This is a sound I used to hear
on the kitchen radios of my childhood,
over the churn of the Thor washing machine
and lunch-hour smells of Campbell's Soup.
I was going to give it pride of place
in my Museum of Lost Sounds,
but it turns out this is not a lost sound,

this is *Canada's longest running but shortest radio program,*
first broadcast on November 5, 1939,
and you can still hear it on the radio every day
("*very little changed,*" though I haven't tried)
if you tune in to the right station
at the right time.
                          —So I have learned,
and was amazed to learn,
but I haven't tried.

This is not a lost sound.
But the child who heard it back then
is a lost child,
and I prefer to leave it undisturbed
in her ears

The Dominion Observatory Time Signal

*The beginning of the long dash*
for that child


iv  SOMETHING WAS MISSING

It was the beginning of dwindle.
No one was in the castle.
Summer was slipping away like a small
snake into a crack between rocks,
too quickly to grasp its bright pattern,
a rustle, a movement
in the corner of the eye
of something dappled and sinuous, fleeting,
cornucopia of smells wafting in
through the summer screen door,
and something was missing now
from what used to be enough,

when did we first notice
it wasn't enough?

A decade now goes by like water.
Kiss it goodbye.

I could get all the way across my monkey bars.
I didn't have to let go half way
and drop to the ground, stirring up
ignominious dust. (After, I'd flex
stiff hands, palms stained with rust.)
And I could jump from the top step,
describing an arc in the air to clear
the bottom stoop
                    and land smack
on the front walk (hands to cement
to break momentum)
bearing the shock and sting
of impact in my soles.

Like a doctor's slap
on the day we first draw breath—

Summer was slipping away,
and the river had begun to run backward.
And I said *Where is my trampoline?*
I said *Where is my toboggan?*
And a little herd of dry leaves
came drifting across my path.
The wind was their shepherd.

## v  MIXED DRINK

A little herd of dry leaves.
They shall not want.
They shall crumble into soil and become
food for next year's greening,
food for green pastures

and the river has begun to run backward,
has begun to run
forwards and backwards,
like an estuary at its widening,
a salt wedge driving inland towards childhood
while freshets of Now press seaward,
a mixing of waters, salt and sweet

(my toboggan got away from me,
went kiting down the slope uncaptained,
light as a paper boat, bumping and bouncing
while I watched from the crest of the hill)

Fill the dark jug of Change
from the river that runs both ways,
and pour our cup.
This is the water we shall drink
for the rest of our days,
salt and sweet,

but we're still in the game, still waiting
to hear our numbers called, our cards are
half filled, we're sticking it out
all the way to Bingo.

*One, two.*
*Buckle my shoe.*

I remember the bronzed baby shoes
atop television sets, next to the
baby portraits in silver frames.
What were they all about?
First of the outgrown shoes.
Like cast-off shells
of the soft pink animal foot.

Auntie Sylvia, back from synagogue,
sank into her favourite chair,
eased her feet out of her pinching Sabbath shoes,
and sighed her last words: *Ah, it's good*
*to come home.* Her heart gave out right there.
The legendary end of Auntie S.,
her memory be blessed. Her card
half filled. Envy her her exit.

Undo your shoes,
before they undo you.

It was the beginning of dwindle, it was the end
of summer endlessness. Something was missing
from what used to be enough,
the cup of summer running over,
summer's full cup. Each day running
out into the bird-loud morning
before sun toppled the blocks of shade,
a barefoot dash across soaking grass
to tilt dew off the seats of the swings—

And later: flat dull metal disc
of my roller skate key. Fitting the sockets
round those blunt square bolts, turning it
tighter and tighter, till it wouldn't turn,
till the skate's metal pincers gripped
both sides of a scuffed shoe
and gave it wings—


vii  TIME CAPSULE

And for a while we flew.

(rhythmic click of sidewalk cracks,
and giddy clicklessness
on blacktop, velvet bands of new-rolled tar—
then to unstrap, and walk on air
the height of phantom wheels,
and feel the phantom tingle in our soles
deep into peachy afternoon)

   *each day running out*

Now it's pedestrian plod, in shoes that rub.
Ay, there's the rub: the chafe
of the quotidian. How many times
can a person make dinner? wash up the dishes?
cut one's fingernails? it is all,
and always, to do again,

while things we didn't do, and never will,
queue up on the wires like birds
and wing off, one by one,

or we remove them from our sleeve
(the sleeve we wore them on, next to our hearts),

retire them to a little box
to bury in the garden (but, what garden?
the garden's also buried in the box—)

And our old doctor's dead.

This is the vestibule where we change
our shoes for paper slippers.
This is the waiting room.
Beyond that door
is the cold table where you lie
under the tracking of a radiant eye,
attended by angels in lead aprons.
Take a number.


viii  RAVELLED SLEEVE

I wanted to write subtitles
for a movie of trees rustling in wind,
for I have always loved the sound
of wind in leaves, the sound of trees
talking to each other in their own language,
and I have always known
that what they say is true.

What did I dream?
Thudding—there was something to do with
thudding but I don't remember
what. Something was thudding.
Something maybe to do with
time?
          it wasn't my heart

          Something was racing—

(In the hospital on the hill
meds are dispensed with dinner
in little fluted cups.)

It was the beginning of dwindle, it was the end
of sleeve-repairing sleep—the start
of a ravelled wakefulness, of lying
with eyes wide open in the dark.
Sudden gusting in a midnight alley.
A clangor of empty trash cans
knocked over and rolling. And a
banging of loose doors in the wind—

> *A box is buried in the garden,*
> *and in that box, a garden's buried,*
> *garden we planned but never planted,*
> *dream of a garden,*
> *sealed in a box of dreams.*

ix  ENOUGH

It was the beginning of dwindle.
Sons towered over us.
Daughters, calling long distance,
asked hard questions.
A blight was upon the maples,
spotting the leaves with tar,
and moths were back.

Rain was falling through the
rusty monkey bars
in empty city playgrounds.

It was the beginning of knowing
we were running out of days.

Something was thudding.
Something was racing.
And the ink was stingy—
late nights so quiet I could hear my
pen scratching paper. Penscratch.
Henscratch. Where's the egg?

End-of-summer windows still open
to let in the night air,
and sometimes I thought I could hear
a different wind stirring the trees,
and sometimes I thought one could learn
to find Enough again,
to let what-used-to-be-enough
(summer's cup running out)
*be* enough—given a few more years.

The truth of it:
summers were never any longer
than they are now.

I sat down on the wooden bench
and undid my shoes.

And I said *Where is my trampoline?*

## FALL ARRIVES

Comes a day when we accept
the imperfection of our lives
and begin to hope
for a perfect death.
Goodbye, my illusions.
Anger of my hunger.

Seat-mates on trains, whose names
we never asked, carry away our secrets
and at the end of summer
comes that change in the light,
when the melancholy that underlies things
suddenly overlays them
like a quilt turned wrong side up,
the plain side with the stitching
there to stare us in the face,
there to be reckoned with.
What is this reckoning?

The flipped quilt of the world.

Then fall arrives, with glitter, with bustle,
like an auntie with a gold tooth.

## BREACH

Always a surge of dark exultation
at the change of a season, a sparking
of memories. Today's:
a dawn walk in the city, sunless dawn
near the end of August, when you stepped
through a breach in a construction fence
to cut across an open lot—a sort of ruin,
rubble-strewn, between standing walls,
down near Chinatown. Smell of the river.
Not a soul in sight. No hint of a break
in the cloud cover—lowering sky,
the breeze damp, even clammy.
You were nineteen.
You weren't alone that day, but you were
alone. The hand you held
was noncommittal, loose in yours,
but it held. Nor did you drop it.
At the same time you hugged to yourself
some kind of inner blissful hard pure
aloneness that felt like treasure. A sense
of having embarked on open waters
in the frailest of crafts.
It could at any moment pour rain
on your bare arms—
You mistook this for happiness.

## GLEANINGS AT YEAR'S END

At a New Year's party
you learn to count to ten
in Mandarin: *yi, ar, sun, sseh, woo,*
*liu, chi, ba, jeow, sheu.*
It remains to be seen what good
this will ever do you. Earlier in the day,
the hostess sent an email
to apologize for cutting you off
on the phone: *I had a dog in my arms*
*as I sat behind the steering wheel,*
and you thought this could be
a metaphor for your life,
though you yourself have no dog,
and don't drive.

## IN THE DREAM IT MADE SENSE

Who *wouldn't* be upset on hearing they'd been assigned to play Portia in *King Lear*? Whose idea was it to bring *her* into the picture? Besides, you wanted to be Lear. You wanted to speak the words *Never, never, never, never, never.*

So there you were, waiting for a bus to take you to Penn Station—a hot summer afternoon, waiting on a suburban street corner, not sure if it was the right bus, not even sure if the bus stopped there. With less than an hour to departure time. How did you ever think you were going to make that train?

Lear is real, if you say it backwards.
Portia declaimed on mercy, but showed none.

In the dream of the driverless car, you're in the back seat and suddenly you realize there's no one behind the wheel. The car is on the highway, easily doing ninety. You rattle the doors, they seem locked from the outside. This thing is going by itself—


Reason is a thin gruel to base a life on.

Stand back from your dreaming.

## IMPASSE

As illness makes us live hour by hour,
revising our day as we go.

As winter plants a great snowy
foot in our path.

As glass baffles the fly.

How rosy can you be
without money?

As war when it comes. If it comes.

A boarding pass for a defunct airline
found in the lining of an empty purse.

Garbage blown up against
a wire fence—held there by wind.

The fence itself.

The slippery skin
between layers of an onion.

Is it the sort of day
to ask a hard question?

*This isn't the right time.*

Suddenly the line goes dead.

We are without a map.

## SEED

And the seed-bunches hung in the summer trees
on branches that swung in the wind,
it was the summer when everywhere you went
you heard the cries of newborn babies
out of open windows, or from behind fences
around private gardens, everywhere you went
there was a mother on the other
side of the wall

And the seed-bunches tossed in the wind
and you remembered the catalpas, their blooms
like spilled popcorn in the grass,
you remembered a dizzy old dress,
some silliness with a mattress on a roof
(no jumping back from memory
on its coiled spring,
jumping-jack memory
that says *Boo!* )
you remembered the chestnut that sprouted
in the children's sandbox one spring,
the seedling you nurtured in a flowerpot,
then in a bucket, then in a dug bed
where it grew to a sapling, then to a full-sized tree
that blossoms now each year
in front of a house no longer yours

And the seed-bunches tossed in the wind
on branches that swung and heaved,
it was the summer that came in the wake
of a birdless winter, first of the birdless winters,
it was the summer when everywhere you went
you heard the cries of newborns, and you felt
how all had changed, how all was changing,

summer of darkening horizons,
morrows gone treacherous,
a world dividing quickly
into King of the Castle
and Dirty Rascal

And you called out in your heart,
for the first time, to one on the way.
*Impending, unexpected, cloud-bound child,*
*you are barreling towards me.*

## LACUNAE

Why am I sad tonight?
As if in answer, the rain:
a hushed rush of summer rain.

What is the wall that divides us
from our shining?
Of what is it made?

Ghosts of old stairways cling
to the brick sides of buildings
flanked by vacant lots.

I want to play back the sound
of my own pen moving across the page,
dotting *i*'s and crossing *t*'s.

## VARIATIONS ON AN UNTOLD STORY

i

The illusion of a social life.
Only a thin sift on big gusts
howling in the dark.
The numbers don't add up.
The sight of thickly falling snow
an innocuous way to edge back
towards "story"—people out and about
but not exactly burdened under packages,
our whole generation's failure
to transmit a framework of values
(what my wiser heart suspected all along)—
just the debris of another numb,
wasted day. A few flakes
in the middle of the night. I want
to be a better person.


ii

Sunshine, twittering of birds—a tender quiet,
the world catching its breath.
Noted, mentally, but not celebrated.
Maybe the only real story, the great
human story, is a speck
in the continuum of crisis.
A piece of faded and threadbare navy velour.
Watching the tiny movements of tiny people—
maybe it's a wish for just a taste
of one of the lives I didn't choose.
We need these markers. The new buds
were a green haze over the trees.
A two-minute meeting in spring sunshine
feels more like a lucky accident
than anything I'm *doing* to get it right.

iii

Not for the ancient temple lost
but for the burden of my past wrongs—
if I pluck one string, the other resonates.
The angel of the West has fallen.
Garage sales all up and down the block.
Wind blowing momentary holes in the tree's
green canopy, to the tune of crows cawing—
suddenly a homesickness for the days
when all of this mattered, for the *way*
it mattered. Sun comes to the balcony yet,
two days after the hurricane you're wondering
about where to go to get your hair done,
yellow leaves clinging to a branch, here and there,
like shreds, tatters of summer—it does not feel
as if this could be the whole story.


iv

To keep my fragile hold on the tricky tightrope,
a flash connection between two or three memories
remote from each other in time—but what?
*what*? It's gone… I haven't kept my promise.
I feel so far from stories. (Speeches now.
A lot of heart-bottoms being invoked.)
Up the tree runs the bobtailed squirrel,
he's a plucky one, he gets by.
The world grows madder, days are trickling away,
bevies of sparrows keeping up a constant
manic chirping—I feel an emptiness
in the middle of my childhood, somehow we took
a wrong turn and entered a backwater.
Streetlamps were swaying on their metal poles
like flowers on stalks. I love these winds.

v

The history of the natural world
is a history of warming and cooling.
When did I first notice that the light,
when spring came, was no longer spring light,
that it never warmed up or turned yellow?
Sun breaks through in fragile spots
that move across the opposite shoreline,
now the lake is just a lake, the pier
a concrete pier—a rather ugly one at that.
The dream was rotten to the core.
The drought in the Midwest continues.
A day of mist and gloom—it is a big
empty ear, waiting, listening.
Real life wears thin from story to story.
*Monsieur le Maire*, "Johnny Flag," is dead.


vi

Still a little bit of that magnetism
in the air. Two gaily dressed women on a bench
with bunches of flowers—I said no, I said yes.
We made a quick getaway. Frequent flashes
of platinum-bright lightning, long rolling peals
of thunder—I should be feeling *released*,
not "bereft." Two dwarf irises have bloomed
in the front yard. Round lamps shining a soft gold
through the new leaves. My glasses are broken.
I see that the most complex stories grow slowly
out of bad decisions and robin-song,
a bit like pulling teeth. We are in the same boat
on opposite sides of the ocean. I would do better
sitting on the street playing harmonica, at least
the long-term weather report is gracious.

vii

We will never get to the bottom
of the story. One forgets how wrapped up
people are in their own lives. Cottonwood snow
thick on the ground in the copses, like fleece,
people packing their cars to leave on vacation,
kids, dogs, waiting impatiently in the back seat.
Certain milestones passed. Where are my eyes?
Strong smells of cooking wafting up to the road
through the screen of trees—sudden, incongruous.
She came back slowly, like the Cheshire cat to its
disembodied smile. He said, "Those are good words,
aren't they—powerful words—*Claim what's yours.*"
It wasn't his usual voice, but it came in reply
to my whistle. (Dramatic cloudscapes in the distance.
Conspiracy of silence in which we were raised.)


viii

All the way home I tried to enforce
my mantra: more *eye*, less *brain*.
The markets rallied for a day,
then dipped again. Is it finally time
to fill the basement with canned beans
and bottled water? What a non-holiday.
Balcony days are over. A strange disconnect,
the brain's way of telling us we are not
a machine. A bad cheque, a frozen valve
in an unreachable space, and we're stuck
in this sinking currency. Last night I read
a story out loud, it had some charm but the end
was confusing. Knowing it's all spilled milk now,
no going back. The bottoms of my feet
are unhappy with the hardness of the floor.

ix

One wants to remain the captain of one's
own intentions. We seem to have left
all familiar ground. That's the limb
I happen to be out on—the blue man
in the green world, who when asked
by the green man what he was doing there,
replied, "Me? I'm from another story."
Full moon, and a bad moon. Ice crystals lodged
in the burlap weave of the stair matting.
A language is decoding itself for me,
oblivious to the bursts of wildness beating
at the glass. A distant train whistle
is echoing in the back of my mind.
For the third morning in a row, geese
flying over—a glorious din of honking.

x

Nothing like a dead man's collection of spare parts
to make you feel the transiency of life. Another
frosty dawn, chimney smoke flying away
in sunlit waves and swirls. Let's get this show
on the road. Out of nowhere, a thought about
where people get off—what makes them decide
to pack it in with so-and-so. *Honi soit qui mal
y pense.* (But the real person, at a distance,
goes on evolving.) Famous people are just people,
like you and me. Found in a flea market: the framed
portrait of a rich family's cherished dog—not a
beautiful dog—but brushed, combed, photographed
for posterity. The dog is dust, the dog's owners
are dust, but this survives—his beauty in their eyes
survives. I should write a story about this.

## CASTOFFS

Poignancy of the discarded.
The armless doll that stares
from the trash heap in spring,
the sagging sofa with the cat-scratched arms,
the love-stained mattress in the rain.
Inside-out umbrellas, broken-ribbed,
flapping forlornly in puddles,
and jack-o'-lanterns after Hallowe'en,
askew on compost piles.

Poignancy even of the intact, discarded:
here, today, curbside by the corner post
(among junked chairs and rust-stained mops)
a perfectly good birdcage
with all the fittings: porcelain cups
for seed and water,
ladders, mirrors—all the bells
and whistles—everything
but the bird.

## WHAT WE KEEP

The last leaves came down in a warm wind
that blew all day on the fourteenth of November.
There were three balmy days in a row—we walked
in the park in the last sun of afternoon. Only the willows
still clung to their foliage, golden weeping willows,
sun catchers. We climbed a small hill. One of us
was in labour.

Do we all cling to grandeur of the past?
The ruins of the Parthenon loom over modern Greece,
and the laws of Temple sacrifice endure
in the synagogue prayer service.

Today a man in his fifties
showed me his first-grade workbook,
and a story he wrote on the reverse side
of a cereal box panel at the age of six,
and his first pair of baby shoes, saved
by the mother who abandoned him as a child;
these things sent to him in a box, decades later.
Proof that he once had a mother who loved him.

## A GUIDE TO MODERN VERSE

Strange heads engender
strange words, sometimes
commit them to paper,
where in black ink they gel,
a baffle and perfume.
No need to be afraid
of darkling words
whose sense eludes.
Live with them a while,
let them grow familiar
till you know their savour,
till savouring them becomes
their meaning, or becomes
as much as you will ever
need for them to mean.
It's about closing the distance
that made them strange.
The way a name
grows onto a baby,
from sheer insistence.

# IT IS NOT IN GREAT ACTS

people don't want a destiny
they want a little house, means
enough to feed their children
a doctor when they need one
new shoes, little pleasures
people don't want a mission
they want a little leisure
to go fishing on a Sunday
to sit on a park bench in the sun
sipping coffee and reading the paper

yet who does not dream dreams
in whose eyes is there not the gleam
of some elsewhere, some promise in the air
summer evenings on a blanket in the grass
when all one could wish for is right there
a ripe peach or two, cherries, the children
laughing as they trail sticks
or float boats on the stone pond
tossing their picnic leavings to the ducks and gulls
sun's orange ball of fire
winking through darkening leaves
then the afterglow, rose giving way
to mauve in the mild sky
a few stars like bubbles

flare and fade
of the ice cream evenings
children outside in pajamas
in the endless twilights
parents on the front stoops
calling door to door, one to another
time of no hurry—a life of moments
we didn't cherish enough

it is not in great acts
it is not in great voyages
what we long for is with us, passing too quickly
it is in the evenings, on the stoops
pleasure of the breeze on bare arms
it is in the wind-waft, dream breath
will-o'-the-wisp
wisps of well-being

**TIMELESS**

A certain kind of quiet in an old barn
deep in the afternoon comes back to me now:
the smell of hay, and little watery
cluckings of chickens, the dust
in church-like shafts of sun through chinks
piercing the dimness. It was a sleepy place
to steal away to, deep in the afternoon,
and catch a breath of peace. A timeless place.
But I remember too the boy
who slipped out at first light
to keep a watch in that same space,
his ferocious patience, and the joyful
face at the kitchen door
as he held up, to show, reward—
his breakfast-table offering—
in each hand a fresh egg,
still warm. That was my boy.
Now boy no more.

## SEGOVIA

The guitarists were sitting around
in somebody's basement room
discussing their fingernails.
They were comparing the length
of their fingernails, they were expounding
upon the strength of fingernails,
they were trading chilling tales
of broken fingernails.
The guitarists were filing the ragged
ends of their fingernails grown long
on one hand only, telltale sign,
badge of belonging to the cult,
and they could not afford tickets
to the Julian Bream concert
and they could not afford guitar lessons
but they had all the records,
they had the music, lovingly transcribed
off records, all by ear, hand-scratched
in India ink on music copy-sheets,
note by painstaking note. They had
the apocrypha, the word of mouth,
the heroes. Segovia was self-taught.

## CAMEO

Remembering our younger selves
in the rain.
Ducking under stairways, sheltering.
Streetlamps reflected trembling
in cold puddles.
It was February or early March,
an early thaw, not yet spring,
it must have been soon after we met;
we were barely acquainted then,
nothing had begun for us yet.
What were we doing there
on Lorne Avenue, that night,
in the rain? Heads together,
whispering. Where had we been?
Going home to separate rooms,
but taking our time.
We were students;
it seems to me now
we were children still.
The smell was of spring.
Rainsound a thin pecking
at the last snow crusts.
Rain dripping from the landings.
We were hushed, listening.
We could not know
the brink we stood on.

## CITY THUNDER

Suppose the two of you
shared a dry biscuit on some mildewed porch
under the spread of alley trees, that lean
their heavy-green limbs
against the crumbling brick
and creak in the
humid weather

each of you thinking of the
rain that comes
to wet the alley dust, lighting
the fuzz of moss that spreads
on the damp packed earth
between gnarled roots and rotting boards

Suppose you drank strong tea
out of odd china cups with unmatched saucers
each of you wondering if the rain would come
(hearing the muffled chirps of dusty birds
huddled in holes between the bricks, or
fluffing their feathers to the
windward, on bent wires)

—suppose, with every breath,
you breathed the dank bouquet of
tumbledown sheds, cat musk
and coal dust—

       then,

what if the rain
came down suddenly, with a noise of rivers?

## SWEPT AWAY

How innocent are lovers
in the middle of their lives,
in the years when their lives thicken
and love, reckless love,
overtakes them like a summer storm.
What can they do but
bow to it, they are like trees
in the wind, lashed and tossed,
they are foolish, weeping in restaurants,
making and breaking pacts,
sending each other poems,
quotations, frantic messages,
pronouncements, promises—it is all
so impossible!—weeping in phone booths,
weeping in parked cars, forever scribbling
a note with a borrowed pencil
to slip under a closed door
—like these lines she scribbles now
to slip under the shut door
of the past, the door they shut fast
on the messy years they've chosen
not to revisit. Just a note to let them know,
in case they're in there, somewhere, still,
she doesn't hold it against them any more.

## SPENT

Afterwards, they slept,
breathing an air
dense with their mingled sweats
and wetnesses,
essence that made their sleep
heavy and pure

Afterwards they slept
the sleep they share
for whom the end has come,
when nothing's left
for lips or eyes to tell
or yet pretend

Afterwards they slept—
and where they lay
spent, sleep took away
the sun, and pleasure went
where pleasure goes when sleep
turns limbs to lead

and drives its wedge
between the sleepers
so they wake
separate and still
and near the edge.
Afterwards, they slept.

## TOO LATE

The power was out when we went to bed
that night, remember? It had been out
since suppertime—one of those late
afternoon thunderstorms
that used to roll through the valley
like a tidal wave. We blew out the candles,
forgetting which lights had been on,
forgetting about the radio
till, soon after we'd drifted off,
it jumped to life, full volume,
(along with the bedside lamp)
for a brutal second—just long enough
to jolt us awake with a dire,
frenetic male voice proclaiming, "*Too late!*"
For an instant we blinked at each other,
stupefied. You lunged for the radio knob
as the room went black again,
and there we lay, in country dark
(so much darker than city dark)
with that voice still echoing in our heads.
*Was* it too late? For what?
There were numerous possibilities.
Even back then, there were numerous
possibilities. The kids slept on, oblivious,
in their little rooms, their wooden bunks
under the flyspecked windows,
and after a moment we began to laugh,
a laugh we can reignite
with those words to this day.
*Too late!*
We dissolved in each other's arms
in helpless laughter.

## A BREATH

Dust and rust encrust
an old fan—last summer's fan,
on its last legs last summer.
One thing among so many
we've meant to replace, and never got around.
And now another city summer's
humid heat is on us—airless nights
in the upstairs room.

The oscillating fan
is like a ghostly shadow-head
nodding to left and right beside the bed,
its motor groaning on the swivel
at rhythmic intervals, a sound
we'll learn, as last year, to ignore.
(Last year and how many years before?)
Rust and dust
are filtered through the blades that churn
the dark, our dark, in which we toss
in limp damp sheets, waiting
to catch the little breeze it makes
on each return. Ingenious device!

The lovely little breeze—here it comes now.
So nice. You couldn't tell it
from a real one.

## KEEP OFF THE GRASS

Keep off the grass?
I won't. Not when the grass
is sweetly soaked and overgrown,
mornings in the park, before the sun
has cleared the tops of trees.
Here's where I leave the path,
strike an insouciant diagonal
through clean green squeak
and feathered swish.

Dew, kiss my toes in sandals
and creep in under the straps
to leave your darkwet stain
on the leather soles.
The road is long.
The day, not long enough.
Oh, but the grass
is summer grass…
Dew, cool my heels.

## THINKING OF MY FATHER ON HIS
## SIXTIETH *YAHRZEIT*

My father surrendered early
to gravity—doubtless more permanently
than he intended, who coined the phrase
while in the service, meaning to invoke
something more like a nap in the summer grass
on a hillside overlooking the river
at "Y Depot," than anything quite so final
as overtook him, father of two, a scant
ten years later. The war over, the outlook
full of promise—rainbow over a stretch
of open road. Invisible "x" on it,
marking the spot where accident
would claim him. My father was thirty
when he surrendered to gravity,
leaving me to grow up in his silence,
in the eye of his absence. Eye
of the storm: my post-war life,
my father's absence in a pocket
of quiet between wars.
A moving eye,
moving the "I"
I would become.

## VILLANELLE ON A LINE FROM
## WILLIAM CARLOS WILLIAMS

So close are we to ruin every day!
A friend has lost her son; another's ill.
And *There but for the grace of God*, we say.

Some throw themselves into their work; some pray.
Some live as though there's no tomorrow. Still,
so close are we to ruin every day,

we know we only hold the dark at bay.
It peers at us beneath the curtain frill.
*There but for the grace of God*, we say.

Music hath charms. And wine. Salves that allay
night terrors—but we waken, and a chill
attends our brush with ruin another day:

whispers of trouble, come our neighbours' way.
How long before we taste the bitter pill
ourselves? *But for the grace of God*, we say,

and *Let us love each other, come what may*.
Brave words, half understood. Until, until.
We skirt the edge of ruin every day,
spared by the grace of God. Or so we say.

## PLEASE HAVE A SEAT

You sit. And the vinyl
chair cushion slowly exhales.
Around you, banter
of strangers—the acid
camaraderie of the office.
Hard bright voices of women
around the coffee machine.
This is their domain.
Here they enact their days
that are not yours.

Who is behind the inner door?
Who, ensconced
on a high-backed leather throne,
will hear your sad petition?
He is The Appointed.
You have the appointment.
He has what you need,
but he is needy too.
Think of him as human while you wait.

So it goes in this world.
Think of him as needing.
Give him a face while you bide your time
there, in your chair,
clutching your requisition and the fee.
And burnish your words,

burnish the words
you'll tender as your plea.

## WHEN WE WERE SLAVES IN EGYPT

Something is nudging you
to nose around in dark places.
Attics and basements. To prowl through
boxes of old letters, old clippings,
news once new. Mementos,
keepsakes. Things saved by others,
things you saved, not knowing why.
By times, in dusty places with low ceilings,
you lift the lid on times gone by.

You come from a people of long memory.
*When we were slaves in Egypt*,
said the grownups, year unto year,
on a special night. And you remember
the year you first were old enough to wrap
your head around that—to exclaim,
*Zeyde! Are you that old?*
*Were YOU a slave in Egypt?*
—to grownups' gentle laughter.
Then the thing explained: *No, not I,*
*and not my father, either—not even*
*my father's father—but each year,*
*each father's father's father, back and back,*
*passed down the memory: our people*
*once were slaves in Egypt, and we make*
*their memories our own. For had the Holy One,*
*blessed be He, not taken our forefathers*
*out from there—then we, our children,*
*and our children's children*
*might still be slaves in Egypt.*
*Yes, even you.* (Momentous, sobering thought!)
—Then the singing; then good things to eat.
*Now we are free men.*

The province you live in has, as motto,
*Je me souviens*, but the people you live among
have other memories. Still, you have
(on common ground) this common ground:
a past continuous, a past as presence.
*Je me souviens.* A motto you can make your own.

## SQUARES FOR A PATCHWORK QUILT

The Queen Mother is dead, it's Easter Sunday,
Israel is at war. That fragile hope I sometimes feel—
like a breath of sweetness from mown grass.

I need a little chest in which to put these poems.
What *nothings* we think ourselves "informed" on!
The numbers are against the West.

*Rough winds do shake the darling buds of May.*
Oh, who can live with this fickle weather? I feel
like one pole of a magnet, a bell without a clapper.


To keep up a steady gentle pressure
on the glassy pond, on a low tripod:
large and small goldfish bright as new pennies.

Ambient voices of summer laziness,
a fork clinking, a distant doorlatch clicking shut,
one on each side of the climbing ivies.

I don't dote on every leaf the way I should.
We grew up in the very thick
of a smoke cloud. I think it is all smoke.


I am thinking about the Big Subjects,
peculiarly fitting to the day. From mortality
to nostalgia. A wind has risen.

No percentage in expecting much from these
utterly ordinary things that women do.
Time to put away the folders of letters.

The problem is on the very edge of cliché:
reticence leaves a residue I only like
when I have removed most of what I put on.

A lone soul in a canoe, outdoorsman, yet one
who reads; a letter-writer. Will the canny
old bastard swing things back in his favour?

Change is afoot in the Middle East.
More bad news on a beautiful day,
a contract dead in the water.

I walked on the mountain in the wrong shoes.
Not at all a joking matter to the parties
involved. The vacation is over.


Memory of my mother shaking a few drops
of milk onto her wrist from the baby's bottle,
memory of my mother still young.

A grand (or grandiose?) disguise for a strangely
idle life, watching the world go by—there is
*one* emotion, a semi-ironic nostalgia for the Now.

(Sun broke through for a moment, just then,
and felt like news, but it had dodged
behind a cloud before I could say so.)


Something is breaking down all our narratives,
something screwy in the stars, a tunnel narrowing,
here and there someone's shovel scraping.

We scarcely are cognizant of the present moment
except as a launch pad for the future. A roof
collapsed this week under the weight of snow.

Morning horses over a trough, a dry cornfield
in the sun—how yellow!—the memories
of being peripherally a part of all this.

A caterpillar dangling from a silken thread
right at eye level in the middle of the path
doing strange acrobatics in the air.

What is happier than a dog with a stick
in his mouth? What was so powerful about
hearing the statistics, spoken quietly, over dinner?

A doorway opening wider onto a polyphony
of grassroots initiatives: a generation
that grew up on the breath of doomsayers.


"Will we wake up one day to some disaster
and wish we had danced while the times were good?
But then again," he says, "who feels like dancing?"

Yesterday's optimism has gone *ploop*, like a
leaky balloon. This train is completely sold out.
The trackside, all the way home, awash in wildflowers.

Something to keep chewing over, that can never
be swallowed or spat out. Stories about nobodies
who don't even know that they're nobodies.


Students are back in the city. One hears them
singing rowdily in bars, it drifts across the dark.
The Russians have taken over an airfield in Georgia.

First debris of autumn beginning to blow in
through the open balcony doors—this morning
a few small dry leaves, a dying bumblebee.

Why do I not know the names of more flowers?
Everything gone before I can write it down.
There was just enough space for dancing.

## AN INFREQUENT FLYER LOOKS DOWN

The backwater of an airport lounge.
Across from us, overweight Americans
are eating ugly sandwiches.

Later I watch the ground recede.
Soon we are so high you can't
see a car unless it twinkles.

All my certainties, if I ever had any,
are out the window now.
Did I ever have any, or did I just
think I did? *All perception is gamble.*

Not a bead of thought today,
nothing but doubt.

What is worth wanting?
Consider the subversive hopefulness
of people who are starting over,
people who have lost everything.
The bankrupt optimism of an immigrant.

Give me a talisman, a charm to keep.
Give me a pebble for my pocket,
something to palm in secret.

Twinkle, twinkle, little car
way down there
running on your invisible
ribbon of road,
what are you running on?

## VESTIGIAL

Bloodgleam in a piece of fake coal held up to the sun. In my childhood home, on the tiled hearth beneath the mantel that was "just for fancy," stood a black iron grate filled with these odd-shaped nuggets of black glass. We used to find real coal sometimes, half-buried in dirt at the edge of the weedy backyard, in a little hill of rubble vestigial of the days of coal furnaces. Chunks of glossy black rock with facets that flashed. Or the dull-black nubs and grey hardened bubbles of clinkers. Both of these were coal, said the grownups, who remembered coal furnaces. Coal in two guises, before and after burning—both forms familiar to their generation, commonplace to them; to us, exotic. How could a rock burn? Real coal was opaque. It was the fake coal whose black hid a blood colour, a rust colour, like a trapped glimmer of burning.

I was born too late to hear sleighbells. Some have told me how magical it was to hear them, across great distances, on quiet cold clear winter mornings: how it was like the sound of the cold, a winter music. So many different bells, each with its own tone and pitch. The coalman's sleigh, the milkman's sleigh, the mail sleigh. I believe in the beauty of sleighbells. Sometimes I even seem to hear them in memory. But the memories are not mine.

Old smelly ointments of my childhood are still to be found in the pharmacies. To squeeze one stiffly from its metal tube and breathe its strong medicinal odour is already, oddly, to feel comforted. Remembered wrap of gauze, ooze-through of yellow paste. The smell itself a salve.

Today I'm rolling pennies. A paint-bucket full of pennies, thirty years' worth of old coppers, many still shiny, most a dull brown, the odd one tarnished black or corroded with a crust of green, its date unreadable. Queen Elizabeth pennies, Abraham Lincoln pennies, the rare King George penny I set aside to keep without knowing why. Heads, tails. Maple Leaf, Lincoln Memorial. Special commemorative pennies, but aren't all coins commemorative? Each bears a date, each is a memorial to the year of its minting. And now it's the end of pennies. They have been taken out of circulation, but you can still exchange them for their value at the bank. Today I'm rolling pennies: scooping and sifting handfuls, plowing this pailful that amassed in layers, season after season, collecting the dust of home—lint and grit, bits of dry leaf, desiccated insect fragments, wings and legs. Silted pennies, leaving their grime on my fingers, giving a whole new meaning to the phrase *filthy lucre*. How many hands have these pennies passed through in their years? They have come to the end of their life here, bound now for the smelter. Today I'm sitting on the closet floor, counting pennies, dropping pennies down little paper tubes. But isn't that life—dropping pennies down the tube? *Getting and spending, we lay waste our powers.*

A pretty penny. Penny wise, pound foolish. A penny saved is a penny earned. A penny for your thoughts. Will the proverbs endure when pennies are gone? My children will remember pennies, the last generation to remember them. Glimmer of a penny when it's brand new; blood taste of copper on the tongue. Their children will find one now and then, dull brown, half-buried in dirt at the edge of a weedy backyard.

## IN THE BALANCE

Fire can kindle fire,
but the vessel removed from the fire
soon grows cold.

The forecast: hiatus, quietus.
Fear for the world.
Where's north now?

This speeding-up of time
will end by slowing us down
if we are lucky.

(Pivot of sungleam on the curve
of the metal stair rail.)

## FAR FROM HOME

As one alone in a far place
awaits letters from home,
she waits for a message
from her absent heart—
waits for her heart
to come to her again
and say its say
about a world gone strange.

She longs for passage.
Longs for a clear
memory of what happened.
She does not know what happened.

The heart's stopping place
is an oasis, but the mind
does not there disembark.
Still, she waits

because she knows the heart as home,
knows it for a stay
against the tuggings of the mind
that never rests—

As one alone and far from home,
she waits for word.
Waits for the heart's word
on where she finds herself.
Waits for her heart to find her.

## THE REMNANT

Blown bare, this tree—
just a *minyan* of leaves
left clinging.
         Now,
in a breath of wind,
they bob and bow.

## BELIEF

If I were a word
what word would I be?
I would as lief
be a leaf—

(on the east side of the pond, by the willows, the water
was so still that a dry, curled leaf-boat, drifting on the
surface above its own perfect reflection, made not the
faintest ripple, pushed to and fro by imperceptible
stirrings of the air

the way sometimes, in a thread of air on an almost
windless day, one yellow leaf turns rapidly back and
forth on its long stem: a single leaf, nodding and
nodding as if by its own volition, on an otherwise
motionless tree—)

these are two mysteries
my eyes have seen
that seem to speak

More than a word,
I would as lief be
one of these leaves

# NOTES

In the Slant Light
   pemmican: Invented by North American Natives, this was a high-protein preserved food made by pounding dried game meat and dried fruit into a powder and mixing it with equal amounts of fat. Stored in rawhide pouches, it was a staple of Canadian fur traders and Arctic explorers.

Reading Marianne Moore on a Train between Cobourg and Kingston
   Moore's poem, "Armor's Undermining Modesty," from *Collected Poems* (1951), begins "At first I thought a pest/ must have alighted on my wrist./ It was a moth almost an owl(…)"

My Shoes Are Killing Me, iii Dominion Observatory Time Signal
   Italicized phrases are from *Wikipedia* and the CBC archives. Broadcast from Ottawa as described, the time signal was, for Canadian school kids of my generation and time zone, the end of lunch hour and the cue to get out the door fast or be late back to class. Since the 1970s it has been called the National Research Council official time signal. Broadcast times vary, and in more recent years the ten seconds of silence were reduced to six, then eliminated.

Variations on an Untold Story, v
   "Johnny Flag": Mayor of Montreal from 1954 to 1957 and again from 1960 to 1986, Jean Drapeau was given this nickname by his English-language constituents. He died in 1999.

Thinking of My Father on His Sixtieth *Yahrzeit*
   *Yahrzeit* (Yiddish): the anniversary of a death
   "Y Depot": a Royal Canadian Air Force holding unit headquartered in Halifax during the Second World War

Villanelle on a line from William Carlos Williams
   The quote from Williams is from "Sunday in the Park" (*Paterson*, Book Two), where it appears as "(so close are we to ruin every/ day!)"

When We Were Slaves in Egypt
   Jewish families tell the story of the Exodus every year at the Passover *seder*, a ceremonial meal at which children's questions are the prompt for recalling a collective past. *Je me souviens*, "I remember," is the motto of the province of Quebec, alluding to the collective past of French Canada.

The Remnant
   *minyan* (Hebrew): the ten-man quorum for public recitation of certain prayers central to the Jewish liturgy

# ACKNOWLEDGEMENTS

My thanks to the editors of the following publications in which these poems first appeared, sometimes in slightly different versions:

*ARC Magazine:* 'A Breath,' 'Gleanings at Year's End,' 'Thinking of My Father on His Sixtieth *Yahrzeit*,' 'What We Keep'

*Canadian Notes & Queries:* 'Cameo,' 'Too Late,' 'Belief'

*Contemporary Verse 2:* 'City Thunder'

*The Fiddlehead:* 'Villanelle on a line by William Carlos Williams,' 'In the Dream It Made Sense'

*The Hudson Review:* 'Spent'

*La Traductière:* 'it is not in great acts'

*Literary Review of Canada:* 'Segovia'

*The New Criterion:* 'A Box of Old Family Photos,' 'Reading Marianne Moore on a Train between Cobourg and Kingston'

*The New Quarterly:* 'My Shoes Are Killing Me,' 'Variations on an Untold Story,' 'In the Slant Light,' 'In the Balance,' 'Timeless'

*PN Review:* 'Squares for a Patchwork Quilt'

*PRISM International:* 'An Infrequent Flyer Looks Down,' 'Breach,' 'A Guide to Modern Verse,' 'Lacunae,' 'Swept Away'

*The Times Literary Supplement:* 'Please Have a Seat,' 'Fall Arrives'

*The Walrus:* 'Impasse,' 'Castoffs,' 'Seed'


I am grateful to the Conseil des arts et des lettres du Québec and to the Canada Council for the Arts for their support at different stages in the completion of this body of work.

Special thanks to my first readers, Marc Plourde and editor Eric Ormsby, and to publisher Dan Wells for showing so much faith in me.

## ABOUT THE AUTHOR

**ROBYN SARAH** has lived in Montreal since early childhood. Her writing began to appear in Canadian literary magazines in the 1970s while she completed studies at McGill University and the Conservatoire de musique du Québec. In 1976 she co-founded Villeneuve Publications and until 1987 co-edited its poetry chapbook series, which included first titles by August Kleinzahler, A. F. Moritz, and others. Author of several poetry collections, she has also published two collections of short stories and a book of essays on poetry. Her poems have been anthologized in Canada, the U.S., and the U.K., and since 2011 she has served as poetry editor for Cormorant Books.